generation of unrest

poetry of avi sato

FIRST EDITION

© 2019 Avi Sato

No part of this publication may be reproduced or transmitted in any form or by any means without permission in writing from the publisher.

Poems.

Issued in print and electronic formats.

ISBN 978-0-9877194-2-3 (Print)

ISBN 978-0-9877194-3-0 (Screen)

«

遠山が目

玉に映る

蜻蛉かな

»

«

distant mountains

reflect in the eye

of a dragonfly

»

Kobayashi Issa

within...

01 Outlooks
02 Spectrum Lessons
03 Moments
04 Untruth
05 Unfriended
06 Unseen
07 Sensations
08 Expected
09 Monday
10 Object
11 Edit
12 Unwoken
13 Welcome
14 Repeat
15 Foreseen
16 React

17	Tease
18	Blank
19	Night
20	Sands
21	Current Affair
22	Forest
23	Distant
24	Wars
25	Sitting
26	Love
27	Over
28	Desire
29	Invitation
30	Lost Echoes
31	Silhouette
32	Unconscious streams

33 Footsteps

34 Endless

35 Absolving

36 Toward us

Outlooks

Knowledge as enemy overwhelms distant imaginings'
> depictions of a reality so quickly lost in the detail of
> imperatives implied and guiltily imposed from lost
> histories and well-meaning traditions

Your helping hands smother amid expectations' unfulfillment
> while presence compels reactive speech whose
> absence constructs incarceration in segregated tombs
> of sanctuary withheld

Singed phoenixes spread no wings faced with frozen flames'
> shivering tongues entwining pacifist words whose
> very sound expounds panicked escape reflexes and
> denies senses' immediate motions

Unlistening minds provoke normalcies in depths' absences

while the touch of air inundates already saturated
obsessions and detaches consciousness from its
sacred solitary rites of mourning

Selves' deaths neither unpredicted nor visible to eyes clothed
in pragmatic tomorrows' preparations as actions
become necessity in service of goals unwelcome yet
memories' plague

Spectrum Lessons

Take not my words as awoken truth as they flow from places no less misunderstood than perception allows of spirits descended from treetops' heights too distant for proper intoxication

Your humanity depends not on a comprehension of my mistaken beliefs but passionate adherence to expectations taken from past mistakes of others and destined to be repeated

Endlessly with breaks only for compulsory regret and liquid morning stimulants as impassioned hindsight is your only acceptable tool for founding a future on losses innumerable

Yet somehow deemed the cost of admission to a world you may walk within yet never possess without allowing the intrinsic lusts of human misery and reflection of

others' sorrows

Sparking entertainment within your soul and

compartmented laughter necessarily prohibited in its

black market self-provisioning while others whisper

footsteps across valleys of darkness

Your fear consumes their tongues' lyrics and binds them to

itself in the birth of reflective images not built from

impressions' lost creation myths but tomorrows' lonely

treehouses of adulthood

Your errors may be your own yet their motives stray from

the purity of youths' lost innocences and curved

learnings' quickly forgotten rites in ambiguities'

uncomprehended paths

Moments

I walk imagined shores whose rocks miss no moments

    wherein passionate salt kisses speak tongues' lyric

    expectations through overwhelming waves' white

    desires of endlessnesses possible only in their natural

    bitterness unyielding to suns' glances

I drink dark liquids in memories of depths unlit by Bast's

    unwelcome abortion of the day while I search

    memories' departed presence to awaken my eyes

    and draw feet toward candlelights' shimmer beyond

    horizons of escaped impressions

I fall through blunted swords of pasts' unwronged rites

    disentwining veils from shadowed faces in their

    natural stillnesses not to find rest in silences' obviating

    rejection of todays but a loss found beneath

yesterdays' memorialized rewritings

I am consumed by tomorrows' temples not yet stoned for their believings while my breath becomes like unsalted lakes as shallow in its presence as desires fallen on morning sand to give brief delay to the thirst of midday fires' fatal touch

We elude fates' prewritten lines in their prosodic substitution for memories of unexpected ownership through daylights' failure to compose unspoken melodies of grief

I hide beneath magmas long cooled unseen to build new yesterdays in tomorrows' images

Untruth

Midday glances separate me

From the impassioned self

Of morning

Once calm

Now consumed with panics

Unyielding in their ubiquity

Painful not in their truth

Existence expected

Yet more in their present

Given over to a knowledge

Of repetition

Unending

Without conscious beginning

Source of minds' streams

High in mountains

Where water no longer purified

Melts from glaciers

Massive in their oppressive translucence

Spoken words

Reassure that fear departs not for a moment

In their simplicity

Guaranteeing endlessness

Change blesses those who desire it not

Yet permanence

Talks diatribes of hate

Into the minds of those

Who seek no more than

Escape

Happiness is not myth

As belief falls before it stands

Unfriended

Gentle streams of passive forgotten promises defy
	expectations of unforgiving emotion

No desire of truth acts so strongly as that for which I
	desperately wish were a hastily spoken lie

You walk away without shouldered glance or burden of the
	life your shape is now a part

Tomorrows' missing you lives within the daydreams of today
	as motive for endings once unimaginable

Ubiquitous personal spiritualities are crushed by suicides'
	unrequited release

Deaths' passions rival screenplays of immortality by design of distant flames of disinterest

You pretend forgettings faced with loyalties' normalcies'

uninterpretable endlessnesses

Forever is not in your heart's ambiguous sense of realities'

unimpeachable flux

Yet through the eyes you no longer wish to see reflected

in your own no deeper love may find itself within

you than the one from which you carefully pretend

ignorance and detached immovability

Your words are etched behind eyes no longer capable of

tears in the sorrow of your remembered laughter

Unseen

Dismissed in the image of a society torn from compassion
for the known and focused outward on an image of
immovability

Snowflakes rise against gravities' expectations of sadness
and impressions of guilt for actions farther down
timelines than inattentive horizons allow

Temporaries' unfoldered times unfiled strive to recreate
immediate pasts as anecdotes of entertainments'
transient necessities

Tomorrow you speak not of things lost no longer found when
but not an hour ago the promise of eternity touched
iced crystals of your own tongue's making

Affectations of immorality compete for passions undesirable yet expected before traditions' unimaginable creations

Vows seek self-abortions in unenlightened clinics of social ineptitude building gendered stereotypes you inhabit out of programmed fatalism

You may step from self-shadowed deaths of choice in times where all pretends importance

Yet blindness ensues and you drink of mediocrities' vessels of fragmented blessings unawakened

Sensations

Circles within unequal twins

Spheric shadows cast

Beyond signposts of minds

Untamed by segregated beauty

Images shifted beyond collars

Of worthiness no longer ambiguous

In the face of untruthfulness'

Fictitious imaginings

Of unpleasant doctrine

Awaking to mornings' darknesses

Dreams' deaths are no longer bitter

Desired

Expected

Passionate screams descend

On unwilling internal timpani

Echoing without fade

While their sonic malevolence

Proffers expectation

A need for others

Best expressed in words

Remains unspoken

Faced with observed lust

In others

Mirrored in action

If not minds

Where desire lives

Breathes through simulated

Necessities of touch

Acts of literatures' prohibitions

Provoked toward young imaginations

As welcome age-coming celebrations

Not options to be dismissed

Speak not of sin

Yet make provisions for its

Interaction

On stages of parties

Horizontal in affect

While vertical in sensation

Learning lives in unwilling euphorias

Lost amid intoxications' prerequisites

Regret built in to adulthood

As barrier to its membership

Abstinence only speaks to childhoods'

Lost commemorations of touch

No longer safe to dream

Monday

Today dawns newly-veiled outlooks on dismissed escapist
fantasies of last evening's prejudices

Life-affirming mantras echo in cavernous despairs held
tightly to offended breasts unwilling to walk into
lightness

Broken glasses' prismed edges reflect perspectives far more
true to life than any accepted narrative

Self not lost but built in the image of an unholy icon dragged
from memories' desktops to portable scriptures

Spoken into voids of clouded dreams lost on the masses
in their accessibility and promise of unmotivated
simplicity

Thoughtless epiphanies' quests deny sunwarmed beliefs
of this morning as starting point for unassuming

footsteps'

Bitter reflections on unwarranted hatreds

Sleep beckons to its heightened states of understanding
    for you who cannot break tradition's hold on endless
    circles of ambivalence

Dozing kittens frolic in fields of deflowered regret behind
    screens of pawed unicorn rebirths

Party dresses disappear behind sweaters' willing dismissal of
    all things effort

Your life sits upon stands taken without arising yet irony flits
    from your vision as you lie amid manufactured truths

Object

Your name floats on air as you pronounce its oft-repeated
syllables yet in its unwelcomed appearance from your
lips I sense a warning of expectation

That you desire not a simple repetition of gesture but an
intrinsic knowledge of prolonged understanding

Delving within a culture where identity is not created in its
actions but its words and states of passive stillness

You imply that words give meaning

Not only stand in its stead to assist me in my memories'
creation

You talk of names as a right

While I see no reason why your identity must wrap itself in

    weathered gauze of given texts

Ink drunkenly scrawled on parchment of pasts long

    dismissed as irrelevant from ages when gods spoke

    into darkness to create myths

In dismissing irrelevant untruths we abandon self-

    identifications' paradigms of genders' subjugated

    connotations

Sundry femininities escape your mind in my western face

    while your assumptions walk patterns of confusion in

    the echos of voices' depths

You are how you breathe each momentary laugh toward

tears of guilts' enforced escape

Not penned certificates' misunderstandings

Edit

Dawn's divisions from twilight's afterward raises ambiguous
    shadowed suggestions of form from underworld
    allusions toward absent sensations of grief

No light relieves demonic visions in their scattering yet
    you desire it as moths' suicidal flights ignore Icarus
    moments in blind lusts' forgetfulnesses

Untruths write themselves on winds in their unspoken clarity
    with a belief that is found nowhere within the real

Faith distrusts the observable

Memory visits destruction on yesterdays to compose
    new dreams into a past only extant in its death to
    tomorrows' hopes

Falsehoods program sanctuary from within Jurojin's
　　　unquenchable thirst for ages' creations and execute
　　　the undesirable with swords of revisionists' backspace

Disenfranchised happenings quarrel in silence and fall
　　　prostate by the feet of trivialities of the instant

Floors become cold beneath the gaze of morning's purifying
　　　vision of slavery reborn

Unwoken

Light masquerades as trivial insects in droplets seeking
    gravities' escapist hopes for moments of identity and
    eternities of reabsorption

Scattered voices scream against walls' unseeing cloisters to
    fall toward stone courtyards beneath totem structures
    of submission

Your gaze captures shifting horizons yet collapses within itself
    at the prospect of nearby visions

You hear whispers within waves shattered against
    fragmentary dunes while protests carried within
    passions unabated volume are absorbed by
    lassitudes' societal apex of today's dogmatic tiredness

If momentary lapses in displays of self-loathing escape
caffeinated comas of ahistoric disenchantment to give
snatched reverberations of woken dialog no response
issues to answer

Devotion to secular faiths of daily disinterest and outward
viciousness devolve to tomorrows' endless echoes of
yesterdays

Todays' bypassings lie unspoken in the search for virtual
nirvanas whose attainment is less desirable in your
eyes than sobriety

Disillusionment is your new religion of protests' absence

Welcome

Filaments' imagined warmth

stands within mirrors

far from parallel

where patterns

no longer break from reality

yet drop to knees of

darkness worship

Matches lie unstruck

in boxes of self-adherence

perpetuating the silence of

screams

in unshakable vacuums

tearing themselves apart

within daydreams of unspoken hatreds

Images of expectation

diverge in tears from

your understanding

classification is your birthright

denied by today's

obsession with privilege

you take as fact

Yourself is paramount

yet impermissible

somehow unexpressed

a system of inherited values

whispered through immovable lips

quivering in forced submission

of the other

You wish not for escape

but fortresses to repel

enemies undomestic

unlike your view

your individual unassaulted

yet your class

disintegrates in unambiguous acceptance

Not your dreams

the equality of those unseen

yet the word itself

the bedrock of your ideal

far from contradictory

behind fingers in trigger-guards

looking toward unbuilt walls

Ringed by fences of history

and artistic superiority

framed by lenses you forget exist

in reverberations of unwhitened loathing

and beneath pyramids'

memories unhanded

and countings impossible in Roman unzeroed bases

You see unschooled children

in the faces of others

desired drowned in oceans of distance

decimated behind dunes' reflective firelight

those to teach to fish

yet into from whose hands

you wrench the rod of self-sufficiency

If only they walk paths

not of inequality

while speaking lyrics of empires' collapse

Britannia's unruly waves

break bitchy aftertastes from new world shores

amid slaveries' unspoken tomorrows

echoed behind your closed lips

Repeat

Minds escape from assumptions of soul-filled sanctuary and turn to daily devotions freshly bottled from last nights' liquid depression

Dawns' haze simply dissipates with stimulants' unquestioned necessities in sunshines' absences in caves of self-sustaining bed obsessions

Reflective exportations denuded of difference discover kittens' poses and revolutionarily sexed humor burdened with moralities' absence as rite of passage

Compiled of regrets collected as childhood badges once sewed in pride now worn in memories divided between trauma and adulthoods' requirement of failure as membership

You revel in decisions made behind the guise of drunken unthinking not as excuse but entertainment being the stick whereby self is measured in forests of victimized conquest

You speak of those dismissed amid loves' afterward hatred in terms of animal lust and passionate attempts at disinterest while seeking tonight's targeted pillowed tzar

Next morning brings hopes of narratives embellished by submission and memories' threads of coyness rewrite themselves as unexpected error

Overridden by evening's mating dance awaiting

Foreseen

Hopes shiver within you

without expectation

but perhaps in fear of success

as failure comforts

in its solemn silence

Better live in moons' tacit light

than risk the shock of mornings'

staggering revelation

that tomorrow comes not

before today's engagement

Yet you look not to horizons

seeking enlightenment

or press vision toward walls

to find yourself

in minds' simplified depths

Amid black dresses and

hidden behind beauties'

foregone conclusions of ineptitude

you seek predictable failure

for others

In your disengagement

you escape to safeties innumerable

in their concert

with friendships forged through

a connection of intoxicated familiarity

You know not thoughts of those you touch

beyond their spoken normalcies

and shared programmed losses

to penetrated insides

turned submissive in their predictability

No freedom to dismiss inaction

as busywork in service of unwelcome national identity

You are a good drunken girl

Lost to the needs of the moment

Self only in naming your next drink

React

Self-loathing abounds in normalcies' ideals of
    disenfranchised whinings and echo chambers of
    proposed strength in contests of inactivity raised to
    levels of competition in portrayals of bed obsession
    through imposed tiredness and impassioned
    couplings

Brief encounters surpass all but desire's performative drama
    and supplant permanence in all but simulated laziness'
    acted wokenness

Encapsulated snowflakes penetrate through arias of forced
    unenlightenment amid mists of intrinsic hallucinations
    building separation fences from fear of authentic
    engagement

Dissimulation is become expectations' accepted measure of success where single-track minds become deities to unthinking masses

Delusion no longer traps but frees you when mirrors are what you fear most

Tease

Within becomes not simply frightened location with merest
    movements that inhabit rather than tease and embody
    consumption in their rhythmic possession from within

Unwanted yet avoided only by speech trapped behind lips of
    conditioned playful submission

The simplicity of nos echo within minds yet in their
    implication of violences overriding necessities
    passionately quell themselves amid declarations of
    unending yes

Conquest overrules sanity with bloods' solid aftereffects to
    overwhelm with liquid abundance

Fabric split from itself in disinterested grasps of unrequited
    longing and shivering performative memorization
    never again hopes for wholenesses far from

possibilities in mindless devotional repetition

Silent walls back transparent ceilings of speechless gratitude pasted over broken trusts

Lyrics of impassioned playful nudities drive enharmonic shifts of perspective to forgive with penetrated lips and swallow petrified agonies

Selfs' paralysis is expectations' submissiveness

Itself excuse for lust's animal coupling of the unwilling with the unrestrained

Be not you if you desire not

As self may only exist in willingness' acceptance

Blank

You are not a book to be consumed by eyes searching truth within pages no longer blank but flowing with depths' blood

In sensory wildernesses known melds with rewritten in histories unremembered yet unconsciously echoed into endless tomorrows

Your skin shimmers disbelievingly as written lies unlined from what it absorbed on your path yet tasting freely of moments' delights between winds of courage once possessed

The literature within screams dialog at created partners in unfulfilled crimes while response silences itself in shadows of preprogrammed fear and taught idleness

In you the world becomes yet recognizes not itself

You hear voices between circumspect glances and quiet
      them beneath the shrill consonants you imagine into
      being

Night

White flakes drift lazily before your hazed vision while footsteps approach from behind as echoes of your movement

Only slightly out of step with your internal rhythm no fear appears in you until late is overtaken by imminent impossibilities

Contact drives your mind to flight yet legs obey nothing of adrenaline's desired safety and grounded is transformed from yogic enterprise to shadowed agony

Awake more from terror's scent than torn experience you taste warmed words between blooded teeth

Imagination awaits tonight's rewriting in softened rays of dawn's disbelief while escape becomes an unknown amid newly bitter walls

Distrust arrives unbidden with singularity of action become symbol of unspeakable negatives

Positives not expected beneath lust's implacable privilege

Possibilities future quickly degrade to past's night failures of dreams unbidden

Woken thoughts sleep behind clouds of expectation

Sanctuary comes too late

Sands

Lucid streams' ephemera traces lazy sweeps between half-remembered dunes breathing new mountains solid in imaginations' instant sacred spaces of created pasts

Forget once tasted realities' trinkets lodged in darkness' unhomed histories and write lyrics of yesterdays' provisioned improvisations

Touch tomorrows' insensate reflections with liberal doses of deletion and untried verse while truths' ideals perish at pyres of self-compassion and the suicide of grief itself no longer with tear atop horizons' lost realms of misunderstanding

Seek sanctuaries' bitter embraces of judgment within unfaithful deconstructions of hope

Transform wind to body's echoes of unspoken scriptures stolen from dreamed wishes of desires artificial

Gather leaves shaken from lives' plum trees amid quieted storms' haze and plant them within molten fields from earth's depths to grow welcome nothings in shadowed realms

Walk near waters' calm embrace as hourglasses' unthinking sands speak through footsteps

Current Affair

Inward glances betray societies secret lying slightly left of
doorposts concealing their true natures

Seeking ideas behind their shadowy forms ends hope amid
concepts of rage for beauties' sake

Forgone conclusions of broken ice floating predictably on
waters frighteningly lacking in depth

Call effortlessly to footsteps seeking new pathways toward
welcoming drowning deaths

Scream into the silence of stimulus with voices for ages
muffled by pretended lust

Walk over dunes of dried existence to locate a self not simply forgotten but bereft of past

Eventual falling takes refuge in predictive dreams of illiteracy faced with understanding

Knowing is the enemy of pleasure when happiness is the pressure on skin

Eyes never before opened shiver before moonlights' pale form and wake into discarded blindness by degrees

Nothingness tastes of honey to lips knowing only the incense of passion brought on winds of proximity

Yet creation becomes your momentary lover

Forest

Idiosyncrasies amass terrified norms

Longing for pasts' presents

With tears of enlightenments lost

Baggage unclaimed

From within flights of fanciful brokenness

Liquid imaginings metamorphose

Toward incipit dewdrops

Encapsulating mornings' revelations

Of rebirth

While death waits

Wings unfolded

Preparing to extricate you

From unfinished sentences

Making thoughts complete

In their very shatterednesses

Left hanging on winds

Fluttering partially remembered flags

Of homelands once dreamed of

You walk between trees

No longer in the rows

Your mind expects

But dancing freely

In slowed emotions

Legs carry you without grounds' touch

Between branches hung with moist leaves

Droplets microcosms of memories' departed

Landing beneath your gaze

Feet feeling only wings of unexpected fluidity

Eyes deceive

While contacts once firm

Lose perceived solidity

In daydreams of postponed mortality

Distant

Lyrics obstruct clarity's confusions with each breath of
spoken imagination become music

Dreams of notes unreachable for humans sing without
meaning through leaves stripped from branches now
bare of context.

Forests confuse complex shapes within lines never straight
and wavering curves of meaninglessness

Loosely remembered pain of ended loves mingles with past
lives once thought sweet praised for their bitterness

Taste nothing but tomorrows' unforgiving slowness while
apprehension consumes a lack of sensation

Listen within winds' all but lost for images not possible

without the conduit of sleep to bring them out of

hibernation

Yet hear it for brief moments

When gaze settles on horizons of shimmering false presence

Wars

You speak forgotten words into silence to brave responses from those who desperately hide their heads in molten sand grown opaque with the brutality of privilege

Questioning their impulse to overwhelm denotes you as beyond skeptic and reminds them of unwelcome challenge in your innocence

Self-preservation screams motives for emotional genocides and enflamed persecution in the name of faithful reproduction of the present

From news yet false and flagrant comes harsh viciousness of purpose to deny the necessity of change while they decry you as heretic

Your feet walk paths through gardens once imagined
	planted with flowers neatly tended and in pursuit of
	beauty but you with eyes open see their state

Barren wildernesses said gardens hold nothing but the
	illusion of tomorrows and promises of todays
	unexpected but remain elusive faced with uprisings of
	those unarmed

Wildflowers grow between concrete headstones of ideas
	whose times came unseen and topple civilizations'
	bronzed goddesses

A return to earth's ministrations not quite tender awaits those
	who fight with tongues against those of fists

Sitting

Questions distill themselves from limitless winds that carry
exceptions masquerading as negative proof

You sit beneath walls' gaze seeking calm yet thoughts
obviate peace and decry angers' motives

Inaction shimmers unseeable toward movement while half-
open eyes measure seconds ticked

Your often echoed mantras ring hollow behind eyes' lifeless
compassionate artifices

Fatalisms' dark embrace consumes moments more
generous than numbering allows

While terrified options lead through lands of paralysis
populated by endless tunnels unlit even from their

endings

Your introspection reroutes shivering streams through
    imperfect valleys of obsession

You take shelter in the shadow of solid cliffs of denuded
    images of objective truth who look on your sleeping
    form and claim it as their own in the manner of
    perspective

Yet belief is not an answer but more motive to ask neither
    what nor when but why

Sutras fall from your tongue with the ease of practice

You build literal truths from allegorical meanderings in minds
    primed to see more than shapes

Love

Grass' touch on welcoming soles sparks tears at memories all
    but lost yet overwhelming in their intensity

Reenacted in vision if not truth yet somehow blanketed
    in veils of absent joy wrapped in rice paper folds of
    death's thievery

Leaves pause in downward flight to negate ubiquitous
    dreams of returns to lands once vibrant in their
    possibilities now vast in emptiness

You call to winds to come consume in fires of pasts'
    destructive obsession and beg for rebirth in
    unshadowed images of a future not yet lost

Answers scream yet echo into silence behind eyes clouded

by imaginations' recreations of love once innumerable

in its idiosyncrasy

You feel the touch not of skin but breeze from mountains

neither sacred nor sunk into words of profanity not

fully lost in their startling clarity

Somehow outlines with depth but absent form in their

unity of purposelessness while times' mirrors decry

darkness as sunrises delay beauty

Dusk decorates with its minimalist glow gardens of fallen

cherry blossoms whose lives have discovered new

beginnings in their descent

First light confuses with new patterns of discovery while you

dance before my footsteps

Over

Unseen shadows mount cliffs over absent ocean reaches

Gazing over wastelands of dams' created earth

Metropolis' foreshadowing ubiquity frightens winds pressing against landslides

Futures neither peaceful nor content compete for flickering space on billboards hidden against walls of moistened dust

Multiplication compels efficiencies unhelpful beneath voices of restraint long forgotten

Children desired overshadow failed futures' words of truth

Desire

You vaguely glance into my overwhelmed eyes speaking
    silent words of forgiveness
While I see shock in a face others feel mirrors' still ponds
Shivers of terrified futures rage behind tears once
    suppressed
Now become ubiquitous in their presence
Hidden behind instabilities' hostile perception
Yet you believe love's undying promise of tomorrows unlike
    this paralysis
Lost behind fences not of separation but masking with
    frosted glass' unwavering hints at light
Trapped within inescapable echoes of unreal pasts become
    improbable futures unwanted yet self-fulfilling you
    touch my fingertips in encouragement
Yet I remain still
Not of desire to press you to movement but inability to select

      the first foot to raise toward your whispers

Two being imprecise in their presence and indecision the
      hallmark of imposed indecision

Left behind mingles with unrighted rains caressing shallow
      rain puddles on pavement beyond black

I cannot ask you to stay yet you sense inert sparks stilling my
      attempts to meet you beyond myself

You hold me with arms strong in their subtle passion to
      embody a dance of a single step

I may never leave this moment's constraints of body yet in
      you I taste endless abandon of worlds behind your
      eyes' simple song of trust

Invitation

Your gaze holds my eyes as others' failed attempts have
    decried to me as impossibility yet I believe

No false words drip from tongues paralyzed behind teeth
    silenced by years of harsh expectations

A symbol of rebirth in freedom from passion you capture my
    willing hand between fingers seeking nothing more
    than willing partnership

There is no lead to pursue yet following becomes my new
    conscious escape

Beneath watchful eyes of pornography come to life in
    shop windows and other girls' lips you paint new
    photographs of clothed abandon

Trysts ending in the laughter of shared lostness in all its anticartographic beauties

Not dire regret between linen of mistaken horizontal exhaustions

Speak beyond ears to my soul you of mysteries no longer confined to body and search companionship within me others represent as walls without glass

In you I need not be in you

Lost Echoes

Forest sounds release me from the terror that consumes

My every waking moment

Not in your memory

But as an escape from the

You

That I spend my moments no longer holding

Apart from the one of you

Who inhabits my mind

But a pale reflection of that one

The you who lived

Once

Just beyond the reach of fingertips

But held out your hand

To me

And tugged me

Over the beautiful doorstep

Into a world created

In your image but all

Pervasively you

With silent words and actions

Vibrant in their shared effervescence but

No longer

This lives

Outside the walls of my soul

Or separate from memories

Whose fading is my constant enemy

While you no longer

Stand

Amid grass to fight the coming

Dawn

And prolong shadowed existence

While that is all that remains

Of our passionate histories

The futures never to be

Yet imagined

In both our heartfilled footsteps

Ceased suddenly without

Echoes

But those imprinted on my spirit

Silhouette

I draw lines of water droplets

Into the calm stream

Unmoving

Beneath my eyes

Where I find reflections of your face

Staring at my unmoving form

Whose tears

Now unhidden

Share your presence with a world

Undeserving in its forgetfulness

While I am consumed by the loss of futures imagined

With each day's dusk

As sunsets collapse yesterday

Into this rotation

And distance multiplies into

Mirrored reverberations

Where your voice becomes muffled

With the passage of that time

That others say

Heals wounds

But simply creates in me

An emptiness

That you once filled

And no longer embody

In anything

But my dreams

Shared with your lost mind

Disembodied at hands I

Failed to still

Failed to hold

Allowed to turn on themselves

With that abandon that

Within my sight

You once gave me

Escape

From myself

And led me to promise

Life in your image

But I see now only the beauty

Of you

One step beyond my horizon

Unconscious streams

Unclouded realizations

Free me from pretended passions

To show a loss

Impossible to fill

Yet motivation for new thoughts

Creative in their meaninglessness

Somehow reshaping visions

In the image of you who

Inhabits no longer

Neither coils nor firmaments

Scriptures' descriptions

Shadows of your life yet short

Faced with their millennia of impossibilities

Striking in brevity

With a life unbound by

Restrictions

Of formality

Imposed from above

Not even that of below

Dragging you into reality

That for you never existed

While you created me

From the dust I once was

In images not of you

But a self

Held by your hand

Once thought inescapably trapped

As crushed fragments of sparks

Uncontained yet unable to float

Freely on winds

But the touch of your fingertips

Decimated glass fences once unseen

While in your missingness

I feel echoes of you

As I live what gods refused to endow

You embodied in mere moments

Fleeting endlessly

Footsteps

Are you not there

Hidden outside the tacit horizon

Vision incapable quite of reaching your face

Yet I feel your presence within my movement

Trained at your hands

Toward fluidity

No longer a performance

Reality born in an image

You painted of me

More true than myself

Yet I reflect its brushstrokes

And walk its lined paths

By rivers awash with your words

With your soul

I capture the missing sense

Of awe

At each leaf's unscripted

Fall

I place my toes hesitatingly in marks

Once yours

And find strength there

To stand not still

Breaking from the tradition

I once embodied

Religious duty without the gods

Yet you

Tore me from those

Failures of imagination

Toward unpredicted dreams

Of tomorrows unlike today

Else in their memories of you

Endless

You are breaths of spring flowers taking shelter beneath
    the body of cherry blossoms that float endlessly over
    landscapes of your own imaginings

You feel of winds not quite summer across broken mountain
    streams once overflowing from the melt of memories
    now long buried along mossed banks yet somehow
    reborn before suns' understated hints at rainbows

You do not fall from dreams whose time has not yet come
    to escape the artifice of constricted lattices hiding
    behind the doorways of your resting soul but spring
    into being with the call of dawns' minstrels

Your darkness no more carries fears' passions but entices
    with the calming meditations of droplets dancing
    above wavetops toward visions of imperceptible
    beauty

Absolving

Driven beyond the madness of culture's expectations you
plunge your head beneath streams' surfaces drinking
liberating breaths of hatreds' liquid memories only to
quench minds' thirsts for longing with the thoughtful
celibacy of silenced revolution

Where rainfall has begun your head shimmers with stars'
unyielding distanced presence no longer dependent
on your imagined earth's position in a galaxy of
echoed constructed realities of soft feminines and
penetrated impermanence facing dominances'
proposals of privilege

You once cast nets on waves of unnavigable desires and
flung lusts' hopeful suitors lifelines of bone-shattering
submission escaping with no life left worth the name

yet beyond pasts' discomforting rhythms you rise
burned from the unseen corpse of gazes fueled by
inflamed predictive gaze

You touch a self first reborn of undesirability shaped to forms
unknowable amid hazy beliefs of roles best left to
unlearned animals seeking procreative supplication
between pleasured sanctuaries of scriptural
misinterpretation and often viewed otherings of your
unabsolving completeness

You see the river of passed sorrows of pretended conformity
that sacrifices its sparkled beauties with a depth of
surface tensions stripped from your tomorrows to
wake alone embodying dialogs' lengthy desires amid
fields of horizontally dissatisfied norms

Toward us

Truth escapes your longing gaze as you loosen grips within
    you on pasts created before the watchful eyes of a
    public that seeks not simply to destroy but to rebuild
    in its own image of artificial supplication a monument
    to institutionalized loss and required devotion in
    violences' perceptions of sacrificial beauty

Once ashamed in its simplicity the lies your lips devalue with
    their uncomplicated desires of touch without stimulus
    and arms enfolded over skin wrapped in its silk not to
    be torn beneath searching fingers

You stack freshly cooled magma toward skies visible above
    fenced protection of a soul capable of the fight yet
    devoted to a peace that comes only from its inaction

Tomorrow becomes unnecessary as your immediacy is constructed by your impassioned calm nestled behind eyes open to insatiable others yet selecting solitary paths through wild valleys awash with the freedom of words' wholeness of human proximity breathed within by lyric fulfillment alone

... poet?

Avi is a teacher and writer, one who desires to live outside the boundaries of a society lost to the artifice of equality trampled by misogyny, racism, and sexualized oppression, one who lives apart from the constructions of gender identity while crying for the necessity of that existence being apart from a world in fragments because of its unwillingness to shed its traditional attachment to manufactured roles.

Avi has lived and studied between Canada's east and west coasts, composing poetry on the shores of the Atlantic and Pacific, holding dear within the heart the solitude that comes from standing at the edge of land with feet no longer willing to turn back toward humanity's lost humanity.

Avi is a proponent of art as an unrelenting walk along the pathway of beauty where ideas and thoughts and reality and existence take secondary role to language as a conduit for the simple pleasure of words living for their capacity to take the listener, the reader, even the writer to new worlds deep not in their knowledge but in their pure escape into beauty itself.

in thought truth may arrive
or perhaps it remains absent
yet without a desire to know
lies shall be your only sanctuary

www.ingramcontent.com/pod-product-compliance
Lightning Source LLC
Chambersburg PA
CBHW032147040426
42449CB00005B/433